The Eye of the Believer

An Intrapersonal And Interpersonal Assessment Of How We Come To Develop Our Worldview Of Life And Those Around Us.

Dr. Anthony Walton

"I must develop the ability to see and know who I am, and who I can become in God, if I am to be the best me that I can be."

Copyright © 2021 by Walton Publishing
All rights reserved.
No part of this book may be reproduced or transmitted in any form or means without written permission from the author.

ISBN: 978-1-7367209-0-5

Walton Publishing
Indianapolis, Indiana 46226

Printed in the U.S.A.

The Eye of the Believer

Looking Forward To and Believing God for a Better Tomorrow

"It is Not All About Me"

Dr. Anthony Walton

THE EYE OF THE BELIEVER

FOREWARD

Spiritual applications born out of the author's personal experiences that are practical teachings relating to the normal and spiritual life of the believer, the author uses many supporting scriptures to illustrate his views.

Dr. Walton is an excellent writer and you will be inspired as you read through this book.

Bishop Byron V. Johnson
Founder and Apostolic Covering
New Wineskin Ministries

Dr. Anthony Walton

Dedication

I dedicate this book to those who struggle in life to identify their true purpose and strive to achieve goals that at times seem to be out of their reach. My desire is after reading this book, you will be able to better understand the reason and purpose for your existence, and know that you have a purpose and you can achieve what in times past had appeared to be impossible.

I also dedicate this book to those who have suffered from any kind of abuse; emotional, physical, or mental. Know you are a survivor and despite any pain, you may have experienced in your life you can and will be an overcomer.

The Eye of the Believer

The Eye of the Believer

TABLE OF CONTENTS

The Eye of the Believer 11
The Motivation for Writing this Book 17
Searching for Answers 21
Fast Forward 29
An Opportunity to Share my Faith 35
What does it Mean to be Blind? 37
The Tragedy Of A Believer Who Cannot See 41
We do not All have the Same Vision 43
Beauty Is In The Eye Of The Beholder 45
The Four Gospel Writers 53
What did the Gospel Writers See? 55
Different Types of Visions 71
Oh Say Can You See 75
Is My Perception My True Reality? 81
Words We Should Not Use /Negative Self-Talk 87
Words We Should Use / Positive Self-Talk 89
Be The Best You Can Be 93
Choosing to See the Best in Others 97
Viewing Life Through the Eye of a Carnal Lens 99
Accessing All God Has For Us 101
Covid -19 103

The Eye of the Believer

What Should A Healthy Relationship Look Like? .. 105
References 115

Acknowledgments

I would like to acknowledge those who have played a significant part in my life. I have had many to encourage me as well as correct me when they felt that I might not have been making the best decisions.

I would like to acknowledge first of all my dear wife Shirley Walton who has supported me and encouraged me to allow God to operate in my life to the fullest.

Secondly, my daughter Christina Alisha Walton has been my cheerleader encouraging me to never give up.

Thirdly my sister In-Law Mary Tinker who with her husband Uz Tinker raised my wife from the age of ten years old, after my wife's mom; Corean Tinker passed. always showing support for me encouraging me that I always had the potential to do great things.

Fourthly to all the countless others who have spoken powerful words into my life, showing me support with their actions, kind words, and prayers.

The Eye of the Believer

The Eye of the Believer

The eye is the lamp of the body. If your eyes are healthy, your whole body will be full of light. But if your eyes are unhealthy, your whole body will be full of darkness. If then the light within you is darkness, how great is that darkness!
Matthew 6:23 N.I.V.

Whenever you or I view the world around us, what is it that we see? One person sees the world as being perfect and flawless, while yet another sees it as being cold and isolated. One person views it as being void of meaning, and another may see it as being full of hidden treasures. Another views it as being an uncaring world filled with heartaches and pain, yet another looks at it as being a world of insensitive and uncaring people. While someone would even see it as being a dog-eat-dog world. Some would see those around them as being caring and full of compassion, others would see it as a world of endless opportunities and possibilities.

However, you view the world we live in, you can be sure some will see it from a completely different perspective.

We often view the world around us based on our individual experiences as well as how we process those events that have affected our lives.

The Eye of the Believer

If your experiences are negative, then your view of life and others around you will most likely be tainted by those experiences. On the other hand, if you were raised in a positive, loving, and nurturing environment, you would view those around you with a more positive attitude.

My various experiences in life have made me more understanding of people and causing me to respect the challenges many have had to overcome to get to where they are.

I would like to share with the readers how what we see and how we process what we see are so vital to the development and growth of one's life as he or she strives to become a spiritually healthy Believer.

How you and I process what we see is essential to a healthy view of life. What we see and how we come to understand what we are viewing must be shared with others for the progression of the Kingdom of God.

Our view or understanding must be accurate if we are going to have a positive influence on those with who we may share our worldview with.

"And He answered and said to them, Go and report to John what you have seen and heard: the blind receive sight, the lame walk, the lepers are cleansed, and the deaf hear, the dead are raised up, the poor have the gospel preached to them."
Luke 7:22 NAS

The Eye of the Believer

I would like to carry you on a personal journey that I had to experience for God to reveal His purpose in my life.

The journey God took me on became an eye-opening experience changing my worldview of life. I would like you to go with me as I take you on my journey and share with you what God has revealed to be. My prayer is that you will gain a better insight as to why you face the things in life that you have gone through and will allow those experiences not to break you but rather to make you a stronger person.

Have you ever wondered why it is that some people find themselves constantly in trouble or just coming out of trouble only to find that they end up getting right back into the same dilemmas they were previously in? Many times the reason for this is because lots of us at one time or another have fallen into the trap of not looking before we leap or what I call "stinking thinking." (I will discuss this further later). As the old saying goes, "Hindsight is better than foresight."

We all have at times regretted decisions we made, while we were so emotionally involved in a situation we were dealing with, to the point we could not see beyond the problems we were facing. Because we were so emotionally involved, we did not take the time to look beyond what we were feeling at the time. Had we not relied on our emotions the outcome would most likely have been much different. We often side-stepped wise decisions by neglecting to consider what the consequences of our actions would be or the impact (our response to what we saw) of our decisions would have on others as well as our future.

All true believers should understand the importance of viewing themselves and others inrelationship to God's purpose for their lives. Many of us are challenged in our spiritual and natural relationships as well as in our finances. Why? Simply because of how we choose to view these relationships as well as the importance we assign to these critical areas in our lives. We should be aware that any decision we make will not only impact us but those around us for years to come.

The world around us, the people who we must communicate with daily, the activities we participate in, how we relate to our brothers and sisters, not only in our assemblies, but our brothers and sisters in other assemblies, other denominations, and on our jobs can all be affected by the way we choose to view them. Furthermore, we are all challenged by the ways we view the various types of conflicts we are confronted with. We must learn to realize many of the areas we havea conflict with are there as an opportunity for you and me to grow. They cause us to have to take a closer look at ourselves and make objective evaluations of where we are in God, as well as our relationship with those whom God has placed in our lives that we must deal with on a daily basis.

The Eye of the Believer

Having a healthy view of ourselves allows us to be able to make healthier decisions and judgments regarding matters in our life that are vital to our growth and decision-making process.

The Eye of the Believer

The Eye of the Believer

The Motivation for Writing this Book

> *"Hast thou not known? hast thou not heard that the everlasting God, the LORD, the Creator of the ends of the earth, fainteth not, neither is weary? There is no searching of his understanding. He giveth power to the faint; and to them that have no might he increaseth strength. "*
>
> *Isaiah 40:28-29*

Some years ago, when I was a teenager, I had a spot in my right eye. I can remember someone saying that they thought it was cute, but little did I know what someone thought was cute was actually a sign of a bigger problem I had not realized was present within my eye.

I don't know how long the problem had existed with my eye or when it first came about. It had affected my everyday life, my productivity, my view of what I saw around me, and yet I was completely unaware there was anything wrong with my vision.

Many believers are dealing with difficult problems and issues in their lives not seeing or being able to realize they have a problem, not to say the least of having an understanding as to the magnitude of the problems. Until someone who cares enough about them to be honest enough to

The Eye of the Believer

point the problem out to them or until the problem is revealed to them by the Holy Spirit.

There are also times when God will use your enemy to call out a character flaw or fault that you may be unaware you have. Often we will ignore or dismiss our faults or shortcomings especially when they are pointed out by someone we feel are not our friend. We will dismiss it by saying *"They ain't doing nothing but hating on me, that's ain't nothing but the devil."* But whether they are hating on you or not, God may be using that individual to expose a fault in you that your friends are unwilling to because of fear of destroying their close relationship with you or a reluctance of telling you the whole truth and nothing but the truth. It's like the saying **"You can't handle the truth"**. And for some of us, that is exactly the case.

I remember going to the license branch to renew my driver's license and when I was asked to read the middle line I could not see anything. It was at that moment, I realized I had a problem with my eye. I could not see clearly out of my right eye. My left eye was carrying the weight of both eyes. I could see out of my right eye but not well enough to read any print less than two inches in size. This was the first time I realized something was seriously wrong with my eyes and that I needed to have them checked. A family member encouraged me to have my eyes checked out by an eye specialist. At that time I was only 17 years of age.

The Eye of the Believer

I made an appointment with an optometrist, who advised me I had a cataract (*a clouding that develops in the crystalline lens of the eye or its envelope-lens capsule, varying in degree from slight to complete opacity and obstructing the passage of light)*, In simple terms, I could not see clearly out of that eye due to the clouding of the eye preventing the light from passing through.

Often Christians, when viewing life will allow many of the negative events that happen to them to affect them in ways that can cloud their view of life and prevent them from being able to see clearly, the light and beauty of God in their life as well as in the lives of others. I wonder how many Christians today are suffering from the problem of having spiritual cataracts.

The Eye of the Believer

Searching for Answers

The question now was how this could have happened to me at such a young age of only 17 years old, and not having any family history of cataracts.

My optometrist referred me to an eye specialist, an Ophthalmologist, a doctor who specializes in the prevention and treatment of this, and other eye problems.

Unfortunately, I did not have any medical insurance at that time, neither did I have the money to pay for a specialist, or to pay to have surgery.

I later found out, because I was a fulltime student at Indiana University Purdue University Indianapolis (I.U.P.U.I.) I was eligible to be treated at no charge through Indiana University's school of medicine (Hallelujah!)

This was the beginning of a long and tedious process to determine the cause and treatment of my eye problem.

I met a great doctor and gentleman by the name of Nicholas Radar who at that time was finishing up his residency as an ophthalmologist at Indiana University Purdue University Indianapolis. He later turned out to be one of the best doctors in

The Eye of the Believer

his field. We have since kept in contact with each other throughout the years.

I was informed the cataract was impairing my vision, and if I wanted the problem corrected I would have to have eye surgery. Needless to say, the thought of me at 17 years old and having to have my eye operated on was quite frightening.

After about ten months of undergoing many tests to determine the cause or causes of my cataract, and the doctors not being able to pinpoint the exact cause, I was informed I would most likely need to have surgery to correct the problem. Even though I was somewhat apprehensive about the surgery, I agree to allow the ophthalmologist to perform the surgery.

The surgery for my cataract was not as simple then as the procedures are today, laser surgery was not available at that time and I had to be admitted into the hospital for about a week following the surgery.

The Eye of the Believer

"And immediately there fell from his eyes as it had been scales: and he received sight forthwith, and arose, and was baptized.
Acts 9:18 KJV

Following the surgery, with the aid of contact lenses and or eyeglasses, I could see things that I had not previously been able to see with my right eye. It was like a miracle. The things around me had not changed but my ability to see the things that were once out of focus, or rather were hidden due to the flaw with my eye, made my vision seem to open up. It was like a whole new and better view of the things around me as far as my eye could see. It was quite refreshing and exciting.

The scales that had been taken off my eye were scar tissues that prevented me from being able to see out of the eye.

When you and I have been scarred by the trials and heartaches of this life, it affects our vision and makes it difficult at times, if not impossible, to see the glory of God. It is not until we allow God to operate on our hearts, (remove the scars and the hurt, and the things that have plagued our lives) that we will be able to experience the refreshing release of God's presence in our life.

"For thus saith the high and lofty One that inhabiteth eternity, whose name is Holy; I dwell in the high and holy place, with him also that is of a contrite and humble spirit, to revive the spirit of the humble, and to revive the heart of the contrite ones."
Isaiah 57:15 KJV

The Eye of the Believer

For the next few years, I was able to see things much better. I was enjoying my new found vision, but approximately two years after my surgery during my routine follow up visit, I was once again informed there was a problem with my right eye. A film had developed from the previous surgery. I was advised I would have to have it removed if I wanted to be able to see clearly again out of my eye. I was told fluid was leaking from the eye and I would have to have what is called a posterior capsulotomy to remove the film. I was told this surgery would not be as intense as the first even though it too would require a stay in the hospital of about three days. I agreed to have the additional surgery.

What seemed to be going right with my eye had seemingly changed over the course of time.

Often God has to continue to work on us over and over and over again. God many times places renewed challenges in our lives causing us to focus our eyes on Him and to let us know that our lives are not governed by our own will but by the will of God. The child of God must always stay in a continual mode of prayer.

We should never get too comfortable with the victories we have already overcome, that we forget the battle or struggles we had to endure that we may obtain these victories.

We should never allow ourselves to get so complacent that we are slack in our prayer lives, our

The Eye of the Believer

church attendance, and our constant study of God's word.

Be self-controlled and alert. Your enemy the devil prowls around like a roaring lion looking for someone to devour.
I Peter 5:8 N.I.V.

And there was war again: and David went out, and fought with the Philistines, and slew them with a great slaughter, and they fled from him.
1 Samuel 19:9 KJV

    We are often faced with challenges and giants in our lives, and just when we feel that we have overcome them we find ourselves facing what seems to be the same or similar problem again.

    The second surgery was also a success and with the aid of contact lenses or glasses, I was able once again to see 20/20 out of my eye.

    I realized after having had surgery to correct my vision that what we see and what we are capable of seeing are two different things. I realize the importance of having my vision tested from time to time.

    There are many things internally as well as externally that can ultimately affect our vision or how we perceive things. These things can in the long run cause our vision or view of the things we see to become distorted if left unchecked.

    We must be willing to call into question what we see or how we view the things we face in our lives; As well as the decisions we make, and the people we allow to influence our life whenever

The Eye of the Believer

these things do not line up with the Word of God. If we fail to see things and the people around us for who and what they really are, we can, and will be, deceived by the adversary.

"Lean on, trust in, and be confident in the Lord with all your heart and mind and do not rely on your own insight or understanding. In all your ways know, recognize, and acknowledge him and he will direct and make straight and plain your paths. Be not wise in your own eyes; reverently fear and worship the Lord and turn (entirely) away from evil. "
Proverbs 3:5-7 AMP

There are times when we must ask ourselves:

- Do I have enough information to make a valid decision regarding the directions I have to or want to take?
- When dealing with others, am I judging this person or matters correctly?
- Am I being too critical?
- Am I being critical enough?
- Is this person adding value to my life or are they taking away from my purpose and calling?
- Do I even know enough about this person or situation to make any kind of a valid judgment about him or her, for either good or bad?

The Eye of the Believer

- Am I seeing the things that are before me for what they really are?
- Am I allowing myself to be led by what I feel rather than what I know to be facts?

Our answers to these questions will decide how we respond to what we perceive to be going on in our lives as well as around us. These answers will have an enormous impact, not only on our present situation but can have an even longer-lasting impact on our future generations.

I would encourage you to take an assessment of:

- What is most important to you spiritually
- Who are the people in your life that really matter the most (that add value to your life)
- What are your short term goals
- What are your long term goals
- What things are you doing to achieve these goals
- What things are you doing that can foreseeably hinder these goals
- Who or what in your life can be considered a distraction
- Who or what might you need to remove from your life

The Eye of the Believer

"Which when Jesus perceived, he said unto them, O ye of little faith, why reason ye among yourselves, because ye have brought no bread? Do ye not yet understand, neither remember the five loaves of the five thousand and how many baskets ye took up?"
Matthew 16:8-9 KJV

We often get so overwhelmed by the challenges we are currently facing to the point we forget about the many victories that God has already allowed us to experience. Our current challenges mayseem worse than the previous ones, but if we compare what we are facing now to where God has brought us from, we would see in many cases the things that we are going through right now are not as bad as what we have already been delivered from.

When we become so overly preoccupied with our circumstances that we are unable to see clearly past them and into our future, we then fail to be able to see the bigger picture.

Jesus was warning his disciples to be aware of the traps of the Pharisees and Sadducees, yet they were so concerned about their physical needs and desires that they could not see what Jesus was really trying to show them. Jesus had to remind them of how he had previously fed the multitudes. In other words, Jesus was saying:

"If I did it once, I can do it again........"

Lord help us to remember our past victories!!!

Fast Forward

Some years later as I was praying, God spoke to me and gave me the title of this book. I kept telling myself that I was going to write this book, but for several more years, I kept putting it off. We often make the mistake of putting off the things we see as not being immediately important in our lives, but many times, these are the very things that should be the most important in our lives. We often put them off because of not feeling that they take a priority over other more pressing matters. The things we put off will in many cases have a longer far-reaching impact on how effective we will be in dealing with what we feel to be more urgent. An example of this is: We know that we should be concerned about exercising and eating a healthy diet but we are more inclined to neglect exercising or watching our diet to go to the movies or to the mall to catch a big sale or something else that we feel to be more interesting to us. I'm not saying anything is wrong with going to the movies or the mall or any of these other places, but simply that we must prioritize what is most important in our life.

We must learn to put everything in its proper perspective. At certain times we may have to put off what gives us instant gratification for something that will ultimately be more beneficial for us in the long run.

There is a term, called opportunity cost, the term states, for us to enjoy one thing we will have to forego or give up the opportunity to enjoy something else. In other words, If I want to secure a good job in the future I may have to spend less time socializing with my friends and apply more time studying in the present moment to receive the future benefits of having to have made the sacrifices to allow me to be able to have earned a degree.

Another example is, if I want to be more spiritually focused, I may have to give up some of the time I spend with my friend and relatives and steal away with God in prayer.

To focus on one thing of importance, I will have to give up something else of lesser importance for a short period or indefinitely. The benefits will be well worth it!

When God gives you a mandate, things will not be complete in your life until the mandate has been completed!

I now realize whenever God gives us a mandate, we must follow it exactly when and how he gives it to us. God will not remove the burden from us until the assignment we have been given has been completed.

The Eye of the Believer

God has to get our attention.

"Now as he traveled on, he came near to Damascus, and suddenly a light from heaven flashed around him, and he fell to the ground. Then he heard a voice saying to him, Saul, Saul, why are you persecuting Me harassing, troubling, and molesting me? And Saul said, who are you, Lord? And he said, I am Jesus, whom you are persecuting, it is dangerous and it will turn out badly for you to keep kicking against the goad to offer vain and perilous resistance]. Trembling and astonished he asked, Lord, what do you desire me to do? The Lord said to him, but arise and go into the city, and you will be told what you must do. The men who were accompanying him were unable to speak for terror, hearing the voice but seeing no one. Then Saul got up from the ground, but though his eyes were opened, he could see nothing; so they led him by the hand and brought him into Damascus. And he was unable to see for three days, and he neither ate nor drank anything."

Acts 9:3-9 AMP

Sometimes God has to blind us to make us see what His will is for us.

Once again, I had purposed in my heart to write this book, and again I put it off. Not because I didn't want to write it but because I was so busy with other things I felt were more urgent, but were not as important.

God had to put a fire under me to get me to write this book.

Again many years later, I found myself having problems with my right eye. I began to

The Eye of the Believer

notice that something was happening with my eye again.

I told my wife something was going on with my eye, I knew something was wrong, but I could not quite tell what the problem was. My wife told me I should go and have my eye checked out, but as many husbands do, I did not heed her advice but put it off.

Two days later, I began to see a shadow forming in my eye, and again my wife urged me to see a doctor. I told her, "I'll have it checked out," but once again, I thought I had plenty of time to schedule an appointment with my eye doctor, and so I put it off again.

The next day my vision was as though someone was cutting slices out of a pie. Little by little, I started seeing less and less until I realized that I had become completely blind out of my eye. I could not see anything out of my eye but light. It was at that time I had no other choice but to take my wife's advice and make an appointment to see my ophthalmologist.

It was on a Sunday when I called my ophthalmologist. I called his office, leaving a message on his voice mail, to my surprise, he called right back and told me to meet him in his office the following day.

Realizing the seriousness of my condition and being concerned of not being able to see out of my eye, I was in the doctor's parking lot the first

The Eye of the Believer

thing the following morning, sitting there waiting on the doctor when he arrived at his office.

It's funny, how whenever we find ourselves in trouble, because of not realizing the importance of doing what we needed to or should have done, that we want other people to move quickly in responding to the dilemma we brought on ourselves.

My ophthalmologist ran a battery of tests on my eye and told me that he would have to refer me to yet another eye doctor, a retina specialist. I never knew there were so many different kinds of doctors specializing in so many different areas of the eye.

When I met with the retina specialist, he told me my retina had become detached and that I needed to have immediate surgery on my eye to correct the problem.

He also informed me that it was critical to correct the problem as soon as possible if I were ever to have a chance of seeing again in that eye. He shared with me that even with the surgery, there would be no guarantee I would ever be able to see out of my eye.

After speaking with my surgeon, I realized the importance of correcting the problem. If I delayed in fixing the problem, rather than staying the same, my eye and the shape of it would get worse.

My doctor told me, had I listened to my wife and came in sooner, he would have been able to address the eye problem with less surgery before the retina had become detached entirely.

The Eye of the Believer

An Opportunity to Share my Faith

And we know that in all things God works for the good of those who love him, who have been called according to his purpose.
Romans 8:28 NIV

I agreed to allow the doctor to operate on my eye under one condition that he would attend at least one service at my church. He agreed.

On the day of the service, I had my iPad with me, and as the nurses were coming to take me into service, I had a Bishop friend who was praying for me over the internet through an application called *Skype,* which allowed me to see and hear the person I was speaking with. At this time the use of social media to communicate was not as popular. The nurses were amazed and said that was the first time they had ever seen a reverend pray for someone over the internet before they went into surgery. They could also hear and see the Bishop praying for me, he was also able to see them. They bowed their heads in silence as we all prayed together.

The doctor was not there when the Bishop prayed for me, but right before we were to go back to begin the surgery, the doctor asked me if I would mind if he prayed for me. I said I would be glad for

The Eye of the Believer

him to pray. I had never seen anything like that before in my life. I could see and feel at that moment in my spirit that God's presence was with me, and felt the comfort of knowing I was going to be alright and somehow God was going to get the glory out of all of this.

The surgery was a success! I now can say,

"I once was blind, but now I see."

It is as a result of these circumstances that God has directed me to write this book. This book was written to encourage, admonish, and reinforce the importance of the natural and spiritual eyes of the believer. To show the readers how he or she may obtain the ability to see past the superficial surface of the experiences they are facing in their life and make them aware of the workings of God in their life in every situation. That they will be able to see through the eyes of God, which will allow them to be able to see God in the midst of their battles and be comforted in knowing and often seeing that God is allowing it to work together for their good.

We are assured and know that [God being a partner in their labor] all things work together and are [fitting into a plan] for good to and for those who love God and are called according to [His] design and purpose
                              Romans 8:28, Amplified Bible

The Eye of the Believer

What does it Mean to be Blind?

For the God of this world has blinded the unbelievers' minds [that they should not discern the truth], preventing them from seeing the illuminating light of the gospel of the glory of Christ (the Messiah), who is the image and likeness of God.
2 Corinthians 4:4 amp

Legal blindness definitions vary but most commonly, if someone is registered as being legally blind they have visual acuity of 20/200 (6/60) or less in the better eye with the best correction possible.

Blindness
- Someone with average visual acuity may also be registered legally blind if their visual field is less than 20 degrees (around 180 degrees is normal)
- The state or condition of being unable to see because of injury, disease, or a congenital condition
- When one's eyesight is so bad that it cannot be corrected back to at least 20/40 vision, but can still see light and shapes, then one is considered legally blind

The Eye of the Believer

- A person does not have to be completely sightless to be considered legally blind.

Having eyes, see ye not? And having ears, hear ye not? And do ye not remember

Mark 8:18 KJV

There are varying degrees of blindness.

We may have the ability to see, but rather allow something or someone to block our vision, preventing us from seeing what we should be seeing.

There are several meanings for the word "see":

- To perceive with the eyes, to look at
- To perceive (things) mentally discern
- To construct a mental image or visualize
- To accept or imagine
- To be cognizant of or recognize
- To foresee
- To investigate or inquire about
- To attend to or escort
- To penetrate to the true nature of
- To understand intellectually or spiritually to have insight

The Eye of the Believer

**Note: In this book, I will in many cases use more than one meaning for the word to <u>see</u> as it relates to the Eye of the Believer.

According as his divine power hath given unto us all things that pertain unto life and Godliness, through the knowledge of him that hath called us to glory and virtue: Whereby are given unto us exceeding great and precious promises: that by these ye might be partakers of the divine nature, having escaped the corruption that is in the world through lust. And beside this, giving all diligence, add to your faith virtue; and to virtue knowledge; And to knowledge temperance; and to temperance patience; and to patience Godliness; and to Godliness brotherly kindness; and to brotherly kindness charity. For if these things be in you, and abound, they make you that ye shall neither be barren nor unfruitful in the knowledge of our Lord Jesus Christ. But he that lacketh these things is blind, and cannot see afar off, and hath forgotten that he was purged from his old sins.
2 Peter 1:3-9 KJV

The Eye of the Believer

The Tragedy Of A Believer Who Cannot See

In those days there was no king in Israel: every man did that which was right in his own eyes
                                    Judges 21:25 KJV

When anyone becomes unable to see or receive a word from God for their soul, due to lack of vision, he or she must then rely on their knowledge or understanding. If that person is not spiritually connected to God, he or she will most likely allow themselves to be subjected to their carnal thinking leading them astray by their own carnal desires, and may never come to know what the will of God is for their life. However, when and if that person chooses to cry out to God for a divine Word, God will send someone to them to show him or her the way they should go. In some cases, God reveals a need for them to change their direction in life or to let some things go out of their life. When it comes to the leader, God may reveal to him or her it is time to pass the mantle on to someone else, or God may even select a person independently of who that person may feel or think would be the one to lead the people of God. Often this is the case when it comes to the succession of the ministry.

The Eye of the Believer

We do not All have the Same Vision

We have been led to maintain the belief and misconception that we all have the same vision or that we should all see things in the same way. But just as it is with our natural sight, so is it also with our spiritual sight.

Many Believers have a hard time working with people who do not see things the same way they do. We must understand, everyone is not going to think exactly as you do or for that matter, even do things the same way you would do them if you were in leadership or their shoes.

We must trust that God will direct his people in the direction they should go. For one person God may lead them over the mountain while for another person God may choose to lead them through the valley.

I would like to take this time to share with the readers what I have experienced while counseling with many of my clients as to how differently many individuals view relationships.

I am transitioning at this point to relationships as I see that as being paramount in the life of the believer. We should strive daily to build

The Eye of the Believer

strong, healthy relationships with those God has allowed us to be connected with.

The Eye of the Believer

Beauty Is In The Eye Of The Beholder

"*Beauty in the eye of the beholder*" has a literal meaning, that the perception of beauty is subjective, what one person finds beautiful another may not.

This saying first appeared in the 3rd Century BC in Greek. It did not appear in English in its current form in print until the 19th century. Various written forms expressed much the same thought.

The phrase was later attributed to Margaret Wolfe Hungerford in her book Molly Bawn, in 1878 (1). She writes "Beauty is in the eye of the beholder." Given this quote and many others, it is clear that many people believe that beauty is defined by the observer.

William Shakespeare was quoted as saying " Friendship is constant in all over things save the office and affairs of love: therefore all hearts in love use their tongue, let every eye negotiate for itself and trust no agent". I interpret this to mean that when we are in love our hearts have their language and we must decide for ourselves what we see as being beautiful and we should not let someone else define what beauty is for us.

When we talk about beauty we talk about what the eyes see and enjoy or find to be attractive to that individual. There are many scriptures in the bible that addresses what we see about beauty.

The Eye of the Believer

Eyes Sayings and Quotes

"You can't depend on your eyes when your imagination is out of focus".

"Where words are restrained, the eyes often talk a great deal."

"The eye through which I see God is the same eye through which God sees me; my eye and God's eye are one eye, one seeing, one knowing, one love."

"You can't depend on your eyes when your imagination is out of focus"   Mark Twain

"Where words are restrained, the eyes often talk a great deal."
                Samuel Richardson

"The eye through which I see God is the same eye through which God sees me; my eye and God's eye are one eye, one seeing, one knowing, one love. "   Meister Eckhart

"The beauty of a woman must be seen from in her eyes because that is the doorway to her heart, the place where love resides. "
                Audrey Hepburn

The Eye of the Believer

"It is often said that before you die your life passes before your eyes. It is in fact true. It's called living."   Terry Pratchett

"Look into my eyes / Eyes are the windows to the soul / Look into my eyes / Eyes, oh you will know / There is no surprise / Eyes, because love is plain to see / Look into my eyes

Ryan Raddon, Finn Bjarrnson, and John Hancock

" Children listen best with their eyes. What you do is what they hear. "   Richard Carlson

"If we could see through each other's eyes you'd be surprised by the many things you may see, things you could never imagine and things you thought could never be."

Poetic Description

"The eyes are not responsible when the mind does the seeing."

Publilius Syrus

"The eyes see not what is before them when the mind is intent on other matters. "   Publilius Syrus

The Eye of the Believer

Biblical References Concerning The Eye:

My face is foul with weeping, and on my eyelids is the shadow of death; Not for any injustice in mine hands: also my prayer is pure. O earth, cover not thou my blood and let my cry have no place. Also now, behold, my witness is in heaven, and my record is on high. My friends scorn me: but mine eye poureth out tears unto God. O that one might plead for a man with God, as a man pleadeth for his neighbour! When a few years are come, then I shall go the way whence I shall not return.
Job 16:16-22 KJV

My eye is consumed because of grief; it waxeth old because of all mine enemies
Psalms 6:7   KJV

"All things are full of labour; man cannot utter it: the eye is not satisfied with seeing, nor the ear filled with hearing"
Ecclesiastes 1:8   KJV

" For since the beginning of the world men have not heard, nor perceived by the ear, neither hath the eye seen, O' God, beside thee, what he hath prepared for him that waiteth for him"
Isaiah 64:4   KJV

" My eye runneth down with rivers of water for the destruction of the daughter of my people"
Lamentations 3:48 KJV

"Ye have heard that is was said by them of old time, Thou shalt not commit adultery. "But I say unto you, That whosoever

The Eye of the Believer

looketh on a woman to lust after her hath committed adultery with her already in his heart. And if thy right eye offend thee, pluck it out, and cast it from thee: for it is profitable for thee that one of thy members should perish, and not that thy whole body should be cast into hell".
Matthew 5:27-30   KJV

"The light of the body is the eye: if therefore thine eye be single, thy whole body shall be full of light. But if thine eye be evil, thy whole body shall be full of darkness. If therefore the light that is in thee be darkness, how great is that darkness! No man can serve two masters: for either he will hate the one, and love the other; or else he will hold to the one, and despise the other. Ye cannot serve God and mammon. Therefore I say unto you, Take no thought for your life, what ye shall eat, or what ye shall drink; nor yet for your body, what ye shall put on. Is not the life more than meat, and the body than raiment? Behold the fowls of the air: for they sow not, neither do they reap nor gather into barns; yet your heavenly Father feedeth them. Are ye not much better than they? Which of you by taking thought can add one cubit unto his stature? And why take ye thought for raiment? Consider the lilies of the field, how they grow; they toil not, neither do they spin: And yet I say unto you, That even Solomon in all his glory was not arrayed like one of these. Wherefore, if God so clothe the grass of the field, which today is, and tomorrow is cast into the oven, shall he not much more clothe you, O ye of little faith? Therefore take no thought, saying, What shall we eat? or, What shall we drink? or, Wherewithal shall we be clothed? (For after all these things do the Gentiles seek:) for your heavenly Father knoweth that ye have need of all these things. But seek ye first the kingdom of God, and his righteousness; and all these things shall be added unto you. Take therefore no thought for the morrow: for the morrow shall take thought for the things of itself. Sufficient unto the day is the evil thereof."
Matthew 6:22-34 KJV

The Eye of the Believer

"Don't criticize, and then you won't be criticized. For others will treat you as you treat them. And why worry about a speck in the eye of a brother when you have a board in your own? Should you say, 'Friend, let me help you get that speck out of your eye,' when you can't even see because of the board in your own? Hypocrite! First, get rid of the board. Then you can see to help your brother."

Matthew 7:1-5, Living Bible

Truly God is good to Israel, even to such as are of a clean heart. But as for me, my feet were almost gone; my steps had well nigh slipped. For I was envious at the foolish when I saw the prosperity of the wicked. For there are no bands in their death: but their strength is firm. They are not in trouble as other men; neither are they plagued like other men. Therefore pride compasseth them about as a chain; violence covereth them as a garment. Their eyes stand out with fatness: they have more than heart could wish.

Psalms 73:1-7

When I thought to know this, it was too painful for me; Until I went into the sanctuary of God; then understood I their end. Surely thou didst set them in slippery places: thou castedst them down into destruction. How are they brought into desolation, as in a moment! they are utterly consumed with terrors. As a dream when one awaketh; so, O Lord, when thou awakest, thou shalt despise their image. Thus my heart was grieved, and I was pricked in my reins.

Psalms 73:16-21 KJV

The Eye of the Believer

I would like to take a look at the four gospel writers as we will use them as an example of how not everyone perceives what they see and the events they experience the same event the same way all the time.

As we examine the four gospel writers we will see how these writers were highly anointed by God, and we will also examine examples of how four different men could have four distinct visions of God but yet be in unison in the will and divine purpose of God.

The Four Gospel Writers

Let us take a look at the four synoptic gospel writers, Matthew, Mark, Luke, and John. We see four great men of God who would all see Jesus not just as a man or another prophet, but much more. They each were given a divine revelation of who Jesus was.

To the natural eye, we would ask ourselves how four men could see the same Jesus and come away with a different understanding or revelation of who Jesus Christ is.

It amazes me today how one person can hear the preaching of the gospel and come away with a repented heart asking *"what must I do to be saved,"* while another person can hear the same gospel message preached and come away with an attitude of having been entertained rather than gladly receiving the word of God, and allowing themselves to continue in a state of unrepentance.

It was not an accident they each saw a different view of our Lord and Savior, but it goes to show us many times our experiences with Jesus determine how we view Jesus as well as what we believe he can do for us, and through us, in our lives.

The Eye of the Believer

When we look at what these four gospel writers saw and how they recorded the mighty works of Jesus Christ, though they seem to tell different stories at times, neither of these writers was wrong. They just recorded what they saw or what was revealed to them as they walked with Jesus. Some would call this their perception, but I would point you to how **God takes their humanity** and uses it to **show us his divinity**. They may have walked with Jesus in the flesh, however, when it came to the things of God, especially the divine infallibility of the Word of God, it is not simply a matter of these writers' perceptions but rather the revelation that each was given of Jesus by God.

The Eye of the Believer

What did the Gospel Writers See?

I would like to take a moment to reflect on how each of the four gospel writers viewed Jesus.

It is important to note the first five books of the new testament books in the King James Version are considered to be historical in their content.

We will start with the Apostle Matthew. To give a better understanding of just how each writer viewed Jesus, we must first take a personal look at each of their personal life as well as their ministry.

The History of Matthew

Outside of what is written about him in the book of Matthew there is very little written about the writer. He was the son of Alphaeus, and his hometown was Capernaum. Before he was called by Jesus to be one of his disciples he was named Levi. He was also known by the name of Mattathias, which means "gift of Yahweh," or simply "the gift of God."

It appeared that Matthew had a sinful past in as much as he was a tax collector. At that time tax collectors were known to be corrupt and often feared by as well as hated by many during those days.

The Eye of the Believer

The tax collectors were said to have paid the taxes for the people in advance and then would go after them to recoup the money that had been paid out. Often they would exact more from the people than what they had paid out. The people would not challenge their authority because their decisions were backed by the Roman soldiers.

What is important to note is the fact that Matthew was a tax collector meaning that he was skillful in keeping records which would seem to support his ability to keep an accurate account of his many experiences with Jesus.

The call of Matthew is recorded in three of the gospels. Matthew 9:9-13, Mark 2:13-17, and Luke 5:27-28.

I have chosen to focus on the call of the Apostle Matthew as he presents it to his reader in the book that bears his name.

"As Jesus went on from there, he saw a man named Matthew sitting at the tax collector's booth. "Follow me," he told him, and Matthew got up and followed him. While Jesus was having dinner at Matthew's house, many tax collectors and sinners came and ate with him and his disciples. When the Pharisees saw this, they asked his disciples, "Why does your teacher eat with tax collectors and sinners?" On hearing this, Jesus said, "It is not the healthy who need a doctor, but the sick. But go and learn what this means: 'I desire mercy, not sacrifice.' For I have not come to call the righteous, but sinners."

Matthew 9:9-13 NIV

The Eye of the Believer

Matthew's View

Matthew identifies Jesus as the Messiah (the Greek chrio, "anointed". He covers a span of fourteen generations. he also speaks of Jesus as the son of Abraham a term that would be endearing to the Jews. Emphasizing his Messianic role, Matthew portrays Jesus as the long-expected and anticipated messiah, the son of David. Showing his life was the fulfillment of the Old Testament prophecies. Seeing Jesus as the King, Matthew focuses on his royal genealogy as the son of David.

Comparisons Of The Four Gospels

	Matthew	**Mark**	**Luke**	**John**
Portrait of Jesus	The Prophesied King	The Obedient Servant	The Perfect Man	The Devine Son
Prominent Words	"Fulfilled"	Straightway	Son of Man	Believed
Cultures of the Original Readers	Jews (Jesus, Son of Abraham)	Romans Action: no genealogy	Greeks Jesus, Son of Adam	Church Jesus Son of God
Outlook and Style of the Writer	Teacher	Preacher	Litterateur	Theologian
Outstanding Sections	Sermons	Miracles	Parables	Doctrines
Prominent Ideas	Law	Power	Grace	Glory

The Eye of the Believer

The History of Mark

Mark was given the name John (Jonanan) a Hebrew name meaning "Jehovah is gracious" Mark was his Roman surname which was said to have been adopted in his later life. Mark was also said to be a cousin to Barnabas. His parents were said to be quite religious which contributed to his early religious upbringing.

Many historians note that Mark worked closely with Peter and wrote this book while living in Rome. both he and Peter lived in Rome. Mark's gospel was to be a brief eyewitness account of Jesus' life.

Mark's gospel was written to both Gentile readers as well as Roman laymen. There are three characteristics of his style of writing. Rapid action, vivid detail, and picturesque description.

Rapid Action-Mark placed great emphasis on the actions of Jesus Christ rather than on words. He quickly moves from one miracle or action to another

Vivid detail- Mark presented Christ in vivid detail as the ever-active servant who lived and worked among men and who did not come to be served but became a servant to all.

Picturesque description- as Mark would describe the works of Jesus he did it skillfully to allow the reader to feel as if they were right there with him.

The Eye of the Believer

Mark's gospel portrays Jesus as being continually active and continual to portray Jesus working in ministering as a servant to others.

Mark's View

Mark sees Jesus Christ as the servant of God seeing his humanity. He sees Jesus as he speaks on and demonstrates servitude

And he sat down and called the twelve, and saith unto them, If any man desire to be first, the same shall be last of all, and servant of all.
Mark 9; 35 KJV

The Eye of the Believer

Key Outline Of Mark

"Jesus Asked The question " Who Do Men Say That I Am"

"Jesus Presses the Claim That He Is The Christ"

"Jesus Reveals His Identity Mainly By What He Does"

The Eye of the Believer

Who Do Men Say That I Am?

"Then Jesus and His disciples went on to the villages around Caesarea Philippi. On the way, He questioned His disciples: "Who do people say I am?"   Mark 8:27   Berean Study Bible

Mark presents a portrait of Jesus that I would consider to be the central theme or main point of focus for the believer.

The question of " Who do men say that I am" was important for the disciples at that time and is even more important for you and me to get a clear view of who Jesus is and what he means to each of us. How you see Jesus determines how you will live for him.

The Eye of the Believer

Four Distinctinctions of Christ in the book of Mark

The Person of Christ:

Peter Confesses Jesus as the Christ:

²⁷ And Jesus went on with his disciples to the villages of Caesarea Philippi. And on the way he asked his disciples, "Who do people say that I am?" ²⁸ And they told him, "John the Baptist; and others say, Elijah; and others, one of the prophets." ²⁹ And he asked them, "But who do you say that I am?" Peter answered him, "You are the Christ." ³⁰ And he strictly charged them to tell no one about him.

Mark 8:27-30, ESV

The Work of Christ:

Jesus Foretells His Death and Resurrection:

"And he began to teach them that the Son of Man must suffer many things and be rejected by the elders and the chief priests and the scribes and be killed, and after three days rise again. And he said this plainly. And Peter took him aside and began to rebuke him. But turning and seeing his disciples, he rebuked Peter and said, 'Get behind me, Satan! For you are not setting your mind on the things of God, but on the things of man.'"

Mark 8:31-33 ESV

The Eye of the Believer

The Followers of Christ:

"And calling the crowd to him with his disciples, he said to them, "If anyone would come after me, let him deny himself and take up his cross and follow me. For whoever would save his life will lose it, but whoever loses his life for my sake and the gospel's will save it. For what does it profit a man to gain the whole world and forfeit his soul? For what can a man give in return for his soul? For whoever is ashamed of me and of my words in this adulterous and sinful generation, of him will the Son of Man also be ashamed when he comes in the glory of his Father with the holy angels. And he said to them, "Truly, I say to you, there are some standing here who will not taste death until they see the kingdom of God after it has come with power."
Mark 8:34-9:1 ESV

The Transfiguration of Christ:

And after six days Jesus took with him Peter and James and John, and led them up a high mountain by themselves. And he was transfigured before them, and his clothes became radiant, intensely white, as no one on earth could bleach them. And there appeared to them Elijah with Moses, and they were talking with Jesus. And Peter said to Jesus, "Rabbi, it is good that we are here. Let us make three tents, one for you and one for Moses and one for Elijah." For he did not know what to say, for they were terrified. And a cloud overshadowed them, and a voice came out of the cloud, "This is my beloved Son; listen to him." And suddenly, looking around, they no longer saw anyone with them but Jesus only. And as they were coming down the mountain, he charged them to tell no one what they had seen, until the Son of Man had risen from the dead. So they kept the matter to themselves, questioning what this rising from the dead might mean. And they asked him, "Why do the scribes say that first Elijah must come?" And he said to them, "Elijah does come first to restore all things. And how is it written of the Son of Man that he should suffer many things and be treated with

The Eye of the Believer

contempt? But I tell you that Elijah has come, and they did to him whatever they pleased, as it is written of him.
Mark 9:2-13 ESV

The History of Luke:

Luke's parents were both Greeks. He was most likely one of the only Gentile writers of the New Testament. Luke was said to have either been born in Macedonia or Antioch of Syria and Philippi. He was said to have been close in age to both Jesus and Paul.

His birth name was that of Lucas a shortened form of the Roman name Lucanus. His studies were in medicine which afforded him a uniques view of the gospel. He also appeared to be a student of history as he would often mention many historical events throughout his writings.

Luke presented himself in his writings as being kind, humble, pious, joyful, bright, and gentle. These are also many of the characteristics he attributed to Jesus in his writing.

One notable point is that Luke referred to the prayers of Jesus more than either Matthew or Mark. He also includes three parables on prayer not found in the other gospels.

Luke sees and sets forth to show Jesus as the perfect man. He reflects on the man who in total surrender to God staying constantly before the Father in prayer.

The Eye of the Believer

And it came to pass in those days, that he went out into a mountain to pray, and continued all night in prayer to God.
                    Luke 6:12 KJV

Saying unto them, it is written, My house is the house of prayer: but ye have made it a den of thieves.
                    Luke 19:46 KJV

Lukes Identifications of Jesus:

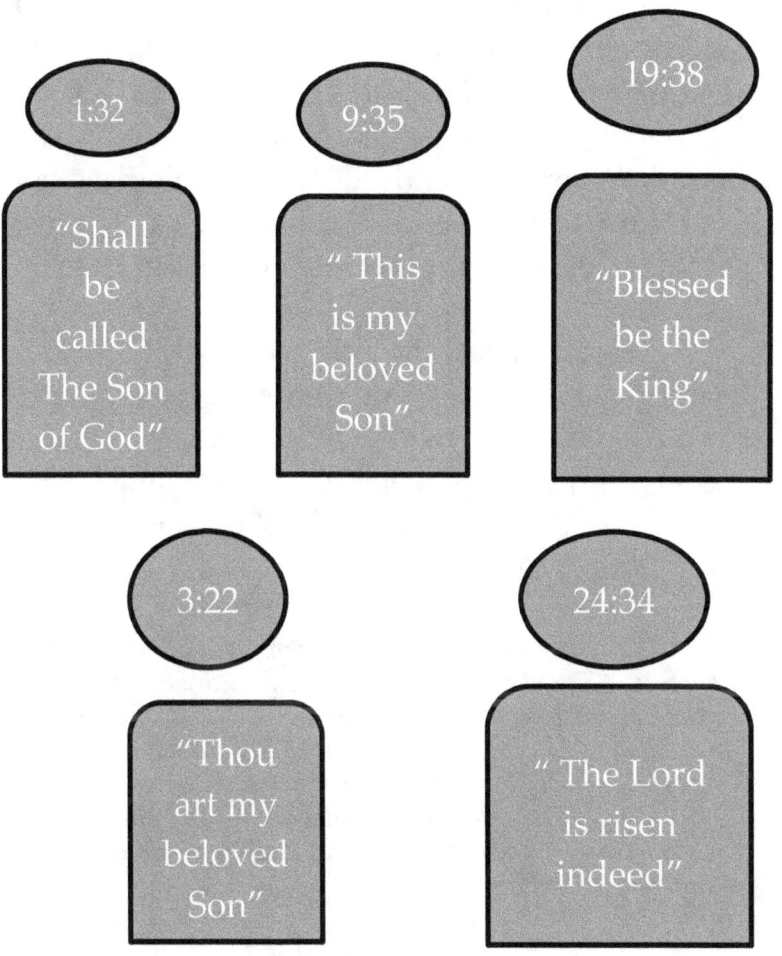

The Eye of the Believer

The History of John:

John, the beloved disciple and author of the fourth gospel, was probably the youngest apostle as well as the only one of the twelve who did not die a martyr's death.

According to the book of Revelations 1:9 near the end of John's life, he was exiled to the isle of Patmos for his witness to the truth of the Gospel.

John often referred to himself as " The Disciple Whom Jesus Loved" some theologians say this is how he viewed himself in the eyes of Jesus, but I like best what the theologian William Barclay has to say:

Barclay states, the title the Disciple Whom Jesus Loved is a lovely title whose meaning did not cross over into our own culture. Perhaps through this phrase "beloved" John wants to highlight God's love and how it transformed his life, rather than his personality or identity.

The writer of the Gospel of John gives himself an odd nickname: "The Disciple Whom Jesus Loved." In other translations, John refers to himself as the "Beloved Disciple."
John was a son of Zebedee and Salom (a sister of Jesus' mother) which make him a cousin of Jesus.
John also wrote three epistles as well as the book of revelation which gives many references to the last days as well as the different church ages.

The Eye of the Believer

John's View

John portrays Jesus as the son of God. He sees and focuses on his divine relationships. He starts his gospel out by undeniably declaring Jesus as the Word incarnated.

"In the beginning, was the word, and the word was with God, and the Word was God."
  John 1:1 KJV

"And the Word was made flesh, and dwelt among us, (and we beheld his glory, the glory as of the only begotten of the Father,) full of grace and truth."
  John 1:14 KJV

Four Main Sections of John's Gospel

1:1	5:1	12:36b	18:1 21:25
Identifications	Conflicts	Preparations	Cries
True Claims	False Charges	Intimate Fellowship	Redemptive Work
Introduction to the people	Opposition by the Jewish Rulers	Instructions for the disciples	Experiences in Triumph

The Eye of the Believer

The Gospel of John "The Eagle's Eye"

William Barclay writes, for many the book of St. John is the most precious book in the New Testament. He paints a beautiful picture of John his writings and his purpose.

Barclay speaks of this book as one which causes the reader to feed their mind and nourish their hearts and can rest their souls.

The writer here gives a reflection of each of the four Gospel writers:

The man *stands for Mark which is the plainest, and the most straightforward, and the most human of the gospels.*

The lion *stands for Matthew, he sees Jesus as the Messiah and the Lion of the tribe of Judah.*

The Ox *stands for Luke because it represents an animal of service and sacrifice. Luke saw Jesus as the great servant of men and the universe and sacrificing for all mankind.*

The Eagle *stands for John because he alone of all living creatures can look straight into the sun and not be dazzled. John has the most penetrating gaze of all the New Testament writers. John gives the reader a glimpse into the eternal truths and the very mind of God.*

The Eye of the Believer

Another Comparison Of The Four Gospels

	Matthew	Mark	Luke	John
Jesus As:	King of Israel	Servant of the Lord	Son Of Man	Son Of God
Readers:	Jews	Romans	Greek	World
Prominent Ideas:	Law	Power	Grace	Glory

The Eye of the Believer

Different Types of Visions

The normal eye:
Able to see both close and distant objects clearly, without distortion or blurriness objects are reproduced as a focused, clear image on the retina.

This should be the state of every believer who has a consistent and committed walk with God. The believer is the person who is committed to prayer, and fasting, church attendance, fellowshipping with other believers, constantly examining and studying the word of God. Maintaining a consistently committed walk, allowing the true child of God to be sensitive to the spirit of God.

Myopia (nearsightedness)
Distant objects look blurry, but close objects look clear.

This is the state of the believer who attends church, intermittently and rather on hits and misses, church and staying connected to the word.the person who does recognize the importance of a more committed life. This is the state of the believer who will not spend time in the presence of God in prayer and will not allow themselves to grow through a constant disciplined life of studying the word of God and fasting. This person may have to

The Eye of the Believer

be spoon-fed because they will only go so far in God because of a lack of total surrender to the things of God.

"I had to feed you with milk, not with solid food because you weren't ready for anything stronger. And you still aren't ready"
1 Corinthians 3:2 N.L.T.

This reflects the state of the believer whenever he or she becomes satisfied with just coming to church and do not see the need for a more personal and intimate relationship with God, he or she will not be able to see the deeper spiritual things of God.

"And when you draw close to God, God will draw close to you. Wash your hands, you sinners, and let your hearts be filled with God alone to make them pure and true to him."
James 4:8 Living Bible (TLB)

Hyperopia (farsightedness)

Close objects look blurry. If the condition is severe, distant objects may also appear unclear. The cornea and the retina are too close together, and the cornea may be flat, causing objects to appear blurry.

This is the state of the person who often questions what he or she sees, but never really appears to come to an understanding of the things of God. He or she may be a constant student of the word of God, but never truly able to get a good

The Eye of the Believer

understanding from the word of God as it applies to their life.

> *"Always learning and never able to come to the knowledge of the truth*
> 2 Timothy 3:7 KJV

Astigmatism:
An uneven cornea causes both close and distant objects to appear unclear. In some cases, a person with astigmatism is also nearsighted or farsighted.

If the cornea is uneven, light rays focus on two or more points, instead of just one. This causes both close and distant objects to appear blurry.

As Christians, what we do not see is just as important as what we do see. Often we are led to believe what we see is the way things are. While many times this is true, there are times when what we think we are seeing is not the reality of what something truly is. So in these situations, we are not looking at or seeing the complete picture.

If we fail to judge and evaluate accurately because of a lack of understanding of what we can see with our spiritual understanding as well as with our natural eyes we can and will easily allow ourselves to be deceived. An example is what many of us may have learned as a child, (because everyone is smiling in your face does not

The Eye of the Believer

necessarily mean they are your friends). I found this out to be a very important lesson.

I'm not saying everyone who smiles at you is not sincere, but often there is more to what we see with our natural eyes. We must realize when it comes to the things of God we cannot simply rely on our natural senses. We should not allow ourselves to be deceived by those who would speak kind words to us merely to lay a trap of deceit and deception there must be another sense that you and I must rely on. And that is the spirit of God. Simply put, you and I must learn to approach and evaluate each situation and circumstance differently.

"Philip ran up to him. He saw that the man from Ethiopia was reading from the writings of the early preacher Isaiah and said, "Do you understand what you are reading? The man from Ethiopia said, "How can I unless someone teaches me?" Then he asked Philip to come up and sit beside him. differently"
Acts 8:30-31   New Life Version

Oh Say Can You See

"And he took the blind man by the hand, and led him out of the town; and when he had spit on his eyes and put his hands upon him, he asked him if he saw ought. And he looked up, and said, I see men as trees, walking."
Mark 8; 23-24 KJV

This scripture illustrates several things to us. First, it shows us that this man was blind. He could not see and had to be brought to Jesus.

There are those in a state of blindness and we who can see, must have a burden that leads us not only to direct the person who is unable to see to Jesus, but we must go above and beyond even if we have to physically carry that man or woman to Jesus where they can be healed.

Sometimes we must go beyond just inviting them to church. We then must be sensitive enough that we can see when our brothers or sisters are in need and create an atmosphere of not judging but of becoming a servant and taking the time to effectively minister to the needs of those that God has placed in our paths.

Secondly, we must realize at times God must place us in a state of isolation for the child of God to see and hear the voice and direction of God. Isolations can seem to be abandonment by others but I have found there are times when God takes us on a journey all by ourselves which causes us to have to be left alone with Jesus.

While we may feel or think our friends have put us down, what has really happened is God has allowed all this to take place so he may have a special private, personal and quiet time with us. When God finishes working on us as well as those around us, many of the friends who we thought had abandoned us will still be there for us and those who God chooses to redirect out of our life will have left us, but we will soon see that it was all for our good.

"And he took the blind man by the hand, and led him out of the town."
Mark 8:23 KJV

Jesus often has to take us aside from others so we can see him, from a position of being uninterrupted by others and able to see what it is he is trying to show and do for us, in us, and through us.

So we must realize our isolation is God's opportunity to allow you and I to see him clearly and to experience a divine revelation of his power through a one on one relationship with Him. A relationship we would not have been able to experience had God not allowed some of our friends

The Eye of the Believer

to leave us alone allowing us to be alone in His presence.

Thirdly, we must be completely honest with God about ourselves and our needs, and even our weaknesses.

The man had been touched by Jesus, but the touch that he received would not have allowed the man to function completely and entirely as he should have been able to or could have been able to.

We must learn to be honest with ourselves in assessing where we are in Christ, our shortcomings, and our faults. It is not until we can see and be honest with ourselves that we can allow the healing power of God to work in us to make us what we can truly become in Christ.

The Christian walk should always be progressive. Even when we come to a standstill must look forward and be determined not to fall back into a negative state of being. But at the same time, we do not have to settle for just anything. We must always strive to do better until our better becomes our best.

God can at any time immediately transform our life and circumstances, but our transformation is often a process.

"And he took the blind man by the hand, and led him out of the town; and when he had spit on his eyes and put his hands upon him, he asked him if he saw ought"
                              Mark 8:23 KJV

The Eye of the Believer

Look what Jesus does:

- He takes him by the hand
- Leads him out of town away from others
- He spits on his eyes
- He touches him
- He questions him
- He allows the man to assess his ability to see

The process took approximately six steps to set up his final blessing. The final blessing came when he was honest with Jesus about how he was and what he was able to see.

"And he looked up, and said, I see men as trees, walking."
Mark 8:25 KJV

Had the man simply said "I am alright, everything is fine" there would have been no complete transformation in his life and no need for Jesus to do anything beyond the blessing that he had already received.

I believe there are times that God would do more in our lives, but we settle for less when we can receive so much more from God. Just ask God for what you want.

The believer needs to be honest about what is needed in his or her life from God. When we allow

The Eye of the Believer

ourselves to be transparent with God concerning our needs we at that time will open up a whole world of endless possibilities for God's blessings on us.

"Now unto him, that is able to do exceeding abundantly above all that we ask or think, according to the power that worketh in us,"
Ephesians 3:20 KJV

"Wherefore I also, after I heard of your faith in the Lord Jesus, and love unto all the saints, Cease not to give thanks for you, making mention of you in my prayers; That the God of our Lord Jesus Christ, the father of glory, may give unto you the spirit of wisdom and revelation in the knowledge of him: The eyes of your understanding being enlightened; that ye may know what is the hope of his calling, and what the riches of the glory of his inheritance in the saints, And what is the exceeding greatness of his power to us-ward who believe, according to the working of his mighty power,"
Ephesians 1:15-19 KJV

Paul writes with a word of encouragement letting them know of the desire for God to work in their life even to a level beyond their ability to see with their natural eye and understanding.

Secondly, Paul expresses his desire for them to obtain spiritual growth and understanding. He shares his prayer that they come to know the love and power of God to operate in their life. He also reminds them how they are constantly in his prayers.

The Eye of the Believer

The Eye of the Believer

Is My Perception My True Reality?

"I believed, therefore have I spoken: I was greatly afflicted: I said in my haste, all men are liars."
                                                    Psalms 1106:10-11 KJV

I would like for you to think about this for a moment, If you were to have been born cross-eyed and were to view the moon daily, your perception would be that there are two moons. This would become your daily reality until somehow someone were to be able to convince you that what you were seeing was not a true reality. It may take corrective eye surgery or simply for God to operate on your spiritual understanding.

Our perceptions become our reality but at times what we perceive is not the true reality, but only the reality that we have made up in our minds through the receiving of incorrect data to our eyes and or other senses.

If we are not careful as well as allowing ourselves to be prayerful, we can get into a rut where we refuse to trust anyone or anything. There have been many times when I have met individuals who have been so hurt by others, they refuse to trust or believe in any person, institution, or spiritual beliefs, because of their past hurts. Unfortunately, they are only able can only focus on the relationships in their life that have been tainted by mistrust, betrayal, lies, and deception. It will take the spirit of God to allow this type of Christian to see that every person who enters into his or her life is not dishonest and not everyone is out to deceive or take advantage of them.

I can remember purchasing a pair of bifocal glasses. It took some time for me to be able to see through them the way they were designed for me to see. I took the glasses back to the optometrist and he had to show me how to look correctly out the lenses. It takes the spirit of God and the preaching of the gospel to teach men and women how they should view God, his creation, and each other.

Many non-Christians and some Christians who are struggling with their faith are like David in the bible that could not at one point see the good in anyone because of being at a low point in his life. He could then only see the negative side.

"I said in my haste, all men are liars"
Psalms 116:11 KJV

For this reason, many men and women choose to stay home rather than go to church.
They are untrusting of any preachers or Christian.

The man or woman of God must carry themselves in such a manner that draws others to the Christ in them. The believer must carry themselves in such a way that causes others to want to inquire of the faith they have in God.

The Eye of the Believer

"Ye are our epistle written in our hearts, known and read of all men:"
2 Corinthians 3:2 KJV

"Let your light so shine before men, that they may see your good works, and glorify your Father which is in heaven."
Matthew 5:16

"The light of the body is the eye: if therefore thine eye be single, thy whole body shall be full of light."
Matthew 6:22 KJV

The eye is the lamp of the body. So if your eye is sound, your entire body will be full of light. But if your eye is unsound, your whole body will be full of darkness. If then the very light in you your conscience is darkened, how dense is that darkness!
Matthew 6:22-23 A.M.P.

How we view ourselves and others is often reflected in the way we talk to others as well as the way we speak to ourselves. It is so important how we speak to ourselves and others if we expect to be the navigators of positive talk and positive actions as a result of what we say.

Let's now go back to the topic of stinking thinking.

"It is the mind that maketh good or ill, that maketh wretch or happy rich or poor."
Edmund Spencer

The Eye of the Believer

According to psychologist Albert Ellis, our upsets are caused not so much by our problems as by what we think about our problems. When our thinking is full of irrational beliefs what Ellis calls stinking thinking we feel awful even when the circumstances don't warrant it. So, how we think about the events in our lives is the key issue. Problems may come and go but our stinking thinking stays with us.

Ellis encourages individuals to practice different behaviors or to look at things from a different more positive perspective." To practice assertiveness skill, to take risks by practicing different positive behaviors, to challenge self-defeating thinking" Corey, G. (2013)

The Bible, referring to the thoughts of a man, says:

"As he thinketh in his heart so is he"
Proverbs 27:7 KJV

The child of God should not, and cannot have a negative or defeated mentality if they want to be winners in life. He or she must see and realize that they are a child of the Most High God and can do all things through the power of the God they serve.

But the Lord said unto me, Say not, I am a child: for thou shalt go to all that I shall send thee, and whatsoever I command thee thou shalt speak
Jeremiah 1:7 KJV

The Eye of the Believer

God does not want you and me to put limits on what we can or cannot do. We must always see ourselves as being empowered by God, enabling us to have the ability to accomplish the impossible.

The Eye of the Believer

Words We Should Not Use /Negative Self-Talk

We often use negative statements to describe ourselves:

- I am too weak
- I am too unattractive
- I am dumb
- I am too poor
- I am unattractive
- I am a failure
- I am not capable of
- I do not have what it takes
- I am not as good as others
- I am not worthless
- I am just not college material
- I just can not see myself
- Nobody cares about me
- I am the only one
- I am too ugly
- I am too fat
- I am too skinny
- I am too big
- I am too short
- I am too small

The Eye of the Believer

The Eye of the Believer

Words We Should Use / Positive Self-Talk

- I can do it
- I am not afraid to try
- With God's help
- I am willing to learn
- I am just the right one
- I am intelligent
- I am strong
- I am successful
- I am loveable
- I have what it takes
- I am beautiful
- I am a child of God
- My father is rich
- I want to be used by God
- I am more than a conqueror
- Greatness is in me
- With God nothing is impossible
- If God be my help

The Eye of the Believer

Greatness is in the D.N.A. of the child of God, but to become effective we must be able to see and recognize ourselves as being great in the sight of God. When God made you, he knew what he was doing, and did not make a mistake.

We must allow ourselves to be able to recognize greatness in ourselves as well as in the lives of others.

I can recall when I was in middle school and we were picking the class president for the student council. Our teacher asked felt in our class would make the best candidate for class president. While calling out possible names we went around the room and I remember my teacher saying "I know someone who would be the ideal person. This person will be strong, positive, determined, and will represent our class well ". Little did I or anyone else in the class know she was referring to me. I never in a million years thought I would be capable of leading anything or anyone. I had a very serious speech impediment which caused me to be very self-conscious whenever I spoke publicly, which caused me to be embarrassed to talk in public.

That event in that year was a defining moment for me. Because my teacher (Ms. Grace Goodman) believed in me. She had enough faith in the ability that I had not seen in my self. She convinced me to believe that I could not only be class president but I could do anything I put my mind to do. From that point forward I developed a

The Eye of the Believer

sense of confidence that I was not aware of before that time, something I never knew I had.

My teacher seeing something in me that I did not see in myself changed my entire life. It was a cathartic moment for me.

The believer must have the ability to see greatness not only in themselves but also be able to see greatness in others even when they are unable to see it in themselves.

Les Carter in his book The Push-Pull Marriage speaks about having a Positive Self-Image. He writes: Explaining how to have a positive self-image is easy, but putting the how-to into practice is often difficult. This requires persistence. Rather than doing exercise, it is a way of thinking. He goes on to state, we have to fix our thoughts on some unchangeable truths that produce a positive self-image even when our feelings and emotions tell us otherwise. Carter, L. (1983)

Let no one seek his own, but each one the other's well-being.
1 Corinthians 10:24

We must, just as my teacher saw something in me, be able to see greatness in others. Too often we are so self-focused that we fail to be able to help others to develop due to only thinking of our best interest rather than the best interest of others.

The Eye of the Believer

The Eye of the Believer

Be The Best You Can Be

"Everything we do should be meaningful and purposeful. If the things we do, do not have any purpose or are not edifying us spiritually then we should take a second look at what we are doing." ~ *Anthony Walton*

I will praise thee; for I am fearfully and wonderfully made: marvelous are thy works; and that my soul knoweth right well. My substance was not hid from thee, when I was made in secret, and curiously wrought in the lowest parts of the earth. Thine eyes did see my substance, yet being unperfect; and in thy book all my members were written, which in continuance were fashioned, when as yet there was none of them. How precious also are thy thoughts unto me, O God! How great is the sum of them! If I should count them, they are more in number than the sand: when I awake, I am still with thee."
Psalms 139:14-17

We are wonderfully made. God makes no mistakes when it comes to you and me. Even when we look at our flaws God sees his perfect work being performed in us.

If I am to write about the eye of the believer and give an accurate account of what we the people of God face as we seek to see God clearly in our daily lives, then I must bring awareness to the human side of the believer. While we strive to walk in the spirit there is still the human element and carnal nature we must strive to overcome.

The Eye of the Believer

Many Christians struggle when it comes to walking in the spirit, and are not able to fully manifest the overcoming power of God. We should not allow ourselves to give in to the desires of the flesh, but rather learn to walk in the power and authority of the Holy Spirit.

The church must teach and preach and even at times have seminars to instruct Christians especially our young people, what it is like to live a Christ-centered life in an immoral society. We must teach them, biblically-based principals.

We must understand not all Christians have been raised in the church, many before they came to know Christ had experienced life from a worldly viewpoint and looked at things such as lying, drugs, casual sex, and many of the things the bible teaches us to reframe from as being no big deal.

I am sure some of those reading this book will say "I don't need anybody to teach me about proper moral behavior" but if we will be honest with ourselves, we all have been tempted, tested, or challenged, by something or someone before, whether we have acted upon our desires or not. Let me state here without hesitation that God can deliver any man or woman from the control of, the lure of, and the enticements of our carnal desires if and when we will submit ourselves to his divine will. However, If we are not taught or not convicted by the Holy Spirit then we will continue in the same sinful path we were on before we received the Holy Spirit.

The Eye of the Believer

For many, the path they were on before they received Christ, was a path of constant partying, drinking, drugs, gambling, and one-night stand after another. Some try to live morally and do the right thing, however were not aware they had the power to not yield to the desires of what their eyes saw.

"Wherein in time past ye walked according to the course of this world, according to the prince of the power of the air, the spirit that now worketh in the children of disobedience:"
Ephesians 2:2 KJV

I do not have the adequate time in this book to talk about this subject, but I feel unfortunately we do not give enough attention to focusing on and teaching our young people how to maintain a well-balanced life.

We must realize the importance of allowing ourselves to come under the control of the power of the Holy Ghost and allow the power of God to keep us.

We must see ourselves as vessels of God andrealize just how wonderfully God has made us. Until we come to realize we are anointed vessels of God, we will never be able to see ourselves for the true men and women of God we have been called to be.

The lack of vision of our true self and purpose can and often will affect our spiritual journey. A lack of moral discipline and acting on improper

The Eye of the Believer

desires will destroy your anointing, and render your witness in- effective.

Lack of vision and not yielding to the spirit of God and giving in to one's carnal or fleshly desires defiles the believer's spirit, saps their desire for fellowship with other believers, and stunts their spiritual growth.

It is so important to know we are all different and are faced with struggles throughout our walk with Christ but because we may be tempted in some areas does not make us sinners, but dwelling on and giving in to whatever our struggle may be and surrendering to those impulses become sinful.

"Let no man say when he is tempted, I am tempted of God: for God cannot be tempted with evil, neither tempteth he any man: But every man is tempted, when he is drawn away of his own lust, and enticed. Then when lust hath conceived, it bringeth forth sin: and sin, when it is finished, bringeth forth death."
James 1:13-15 KJV

Choosing to See the Best in Others

How we choose to view others is an individual decision. There are times we can misjudge others who are for us and in doing so will do them and ourselves a disservice. The question we must ask ourselves is "What are the basis or guidelines we use to judge others?"

It has been said that the church is the only body that kills its wounded. We often misjudge people without even giving ourselves a chance to get to know them.

I have had people who have told me of their dislike for someone, and when I asked them why they did not like the other person, they could not give me a good reason. Often it is simply their perception of that person that comes as a result of some unknown personal reason for not liking the other person.

We must learn to choose to see the best in other people or we will be guilty of judging others by a false standard we have created in our minds.

The Eye of the Believer

"Do not judge and criticize and condemn others unfairly with an attitude of self-righteous superiority as though assuming the office of a judge, so that you will not be judged unfairly."
Matthew 7:1 AMP

The Eye of the Believer

Viewing Life Through the Eye of a Carnal Lens

And there came a man of God, and spake unto the king of Israel, and said, thus saith the Lord, because the Syrians have said, the Lord is God of the hills, but he is not God of the valleys, therefore will I deliver this entire great multitude into thine hand, and ye shall know that I am the Lord.
1 Kings 20-27-28 KJV

The book of I Kings tells us of the story of King Benhadad who failed to see the God of Israel as an omnipresent God. He saw God as being a God that would only give Israel victory in the hills. What a mistake it is when you or I chose to put limits on God. It is easy for us to believe God can bless others, but we are often doubtful when it comes to believing God for what we need. We believe God can deliver others out of trouble, but then when we find ourselves in need we fail to realize the same God that blesses and delivers others out of their storms, is the same God that can and will bless and deliver you and me. God is not only a keeper but a healer, a deliverer, and a way maker. We serve a God that can not only pour out His anointing on us in church, but he can and desires to bless our personal and financial life supernaturally.

The Eye of the Believer

God can bless us with a new home, land, and money in the bank, influence, peace of mind, and favor. Christians should never only view God as being one dimensional.

King Benhadad looked at the greatness of his armies and saw the smallness of the armies of Israel and trusted in what he saw with His natural eyes. He believed that he would defeat the armies of Israel if only he were to fight them in the valley.

Many make the mistake of feeling God is only with us when they are on the mountain top, but fail to realize that **God does not cease to be God when we are in the valley**. Whenever you and I find ourselves facing difficult challenges we must recognize, God is not limited by the valleys in our life.

God sends a word to the king of Israel and tells him because king Benhadad limited God, and could only see the God of Israel as a deliver in their hills, he would show them that what Benehadad had not seen or recognize was the greatness of God's power that was able to go beyond what he could see with his human eyes. God allowed the Syrian armies to be defeated in the valley. What a mighty God we serve.

"And there came a man of God, and spake unto the king of Israel, and said, Thus saith the LORD, Because the Syrians have said, The LORD is God of the hills, but he is not God of the valleys, therefore will I deliver all this great multitude into thine hand, and ye shall know that I am the LORD."

1 Kings 20:28

The Eye of the Believer

Accessing All God Has For Us

We as believers can access far more from our heavenly father than what we can ever see or imagine.

"I must develop the ability to see and know who I am and who I can become in God if I am to be the best me that I can be."   ~ *Anthony Walton*

I am persuaded that God wants to show you and me the greatness of his power and has ordained our marriages, our families, our finances, our health, and every other area of our lives to be blessed.

In all my experiences and challenges that I have had to encounter throughout my life, they have all taught me to put my trust in God and to seek after him so that I may be able to see things in the light of God's perfect and divine will.

I speak blessings over your life, and encourage you to do as the psalmist says;

"O' taste and see that the LORD is good: blessed is the man that trusteth in him."
                                        Psalms 34:8

The Eye of the Believer

Covid -19

When I first began writing this book Covid-19 had not been thought of in the US, at least not as it is currently affecting millions of people.

This has been quite an eye-opening experience for me as I watch and listen to how many perceive the level of threat this disease is to our country and our economy.

Our president at that time had stated that the disease will just magically disappear and by April we will all be in church for Easter. While I prayed that this would happen, the CDC (Department of Disease Control) viewed it as a disease that should cause alarm for all Americans as they have recommended we all should be taking the utmost precautions.

Depending on what views you choose to accept, will greatly impact how you will be affected by the disease.

I realized it is not only important how you view things that have an impact on your life, but it is equally important, how those who you receive your information from view life.

I would encourage the readers to exercise extreme caution and judgment when deciding their

The Eye of the Believer

health in the face of current situations or any such pandemic we may be facing in the future. There is an old saying I heard as a child " An ounce of prevention is worth a pound of cure". In other words, one should be over-prepared rather than under-prepared. This can also be stated as it is better to go out of your way to be a little extra cautious than to not go out of your way and wish you had gone out of your way and spend more time recovering from what you should have done.

What Should A Healthy Relationship Look Like?

Being a Marriage and Family Therapist it is important to address the subject of what a healthy relationship should look like

It is important to examine how we view relationships in and out of the church. I will attempt to address this both from a spiritual as well as a natural point of view.

Focusing on my own experiences, I remember when I first gave my life to Christ I was so excited about the changes God was making in me, I wanted to give up everything and everybody that reminded me of my old way of living.

" Therefore if any man be in Christ, he is a new creature: old things are passed away; behold, all things are become new."
2 Corinthians 5:17 KJV

I literally took this verse to heart. I saw myself as wanting to be the best Christian I could be and thought it was important that I broke off all relationships with what the scripture refers to as "The World".

I began pulling away from many friends with who I had built long-lasting friendships. I thought if

The Eye of the Believer

I were to continue in those relationships then it would hinder my relationship with God. I thought about the scripture:

"Love not the world, neither the things that are in the world. If any man love the world the love of the Father is not in him. "For all that is in the world, the lust of the flesh, and the lust of the eyes, and the pride of life, is not of the Father but is of the world."
1 John 2:15-16 KJV

I believed some level of separating myself from those individuals was the best thing I could have done for myself at the time. As I look back I realize I did not have to completely separate myself.

" I have given them your word. And the world hates them because they do not belong to the world, just as I do not belong to the world. I'm not asking you to take them out of the world, but to keep them safe from the evil one."
John 17:14-15 New Living Bible

While to a certain extent it is important as a new believer to govern wisely who he or she spends time with, we must have balance in our life. While I separated myself from many of my non-Christian friends, I eventually came to understand that while I was separating from them I was not allowing myself to be effective as a Christian. If we completely separate ourselves from others, how will they be able to see and know the change that has taken place in our life?

The Eye of the Believer

"Ye are the light of the world. A city that is set on an hill cannot be hid. Neither do men light a candle, and put it under a bushel, but on a candlestick; and it giveth light unto all that are in the house. Let your light so shine before men, that they may see your good works, and glorify your Father which is in heaven."
Matthew 5:14-16, KJV

I later came to understand the Christian life is about building healthy relationships. It is not about separation and isolation unless it is for a time and period to draw closer to God so that when you come out your light shines even brighter in a dark world.

"And it came to pass, that, as Jesus sat at meat in his house, many publicans and sinners sat also together with Jesus and his disciples: for there were many, and they followed him. And when the scribes and Pharisees saw him eat with publicans and sinners, they said unto his disciples, How is it that he eateth and drinketh with publicans and sinners? When Jesus heard it, he saith unto them, They that are whole have no need of the physician, but they that are sick: I came not to call the righteous, but sinners to repentance"
Mark 2:15-17 KJV

When it comes to our relationship with non-believer we must have a heart of compassion and not be judgmental trying to shame them into changing their life, but show them enough of God's love that inspires them to want to change. Be willing to share with them the love and compassion that you have received from Christ that became the cause of the change in your life.

The Eye of the Believer

"Or despisest thou the riches of his goodness and forbearance and longsuffering; not knowing that the goodness of God leadeth thee to repentance?"
Romans 2:4 KJV

I often heard the saying "We are so heavenly minded that we are no earthly good" I would like to challenge that thinking. If we are truly heavenly minded we then would think and operate in the spirit of God and wisdom. The problem is often we err because we have a misunderstanding of how we are to relate to and interact with others.

In my book *The Window To Understanding and Building Healthy Relationships*, I write concerning what women wished men knew about women " Women wish men knew the importance of just listening. They do not have to try to solve all their problems but be there with a supportive listening ear" Walton, A., Ph.D. (2018). If we would apply this same principle to those who God has placed in our paths as we journey through this life instead of judging them, and if we would just take the time to listen to them and hear their hurt, Oh, what a difference it would make in their life.

In the book Effective Biblical Counseling, Larry Crabb writes "People have one basic personal need that requires two kinds of input for its satisfaction. The most basic need is a sense of personal worth, and acceptance of oneself as a whole. The two required inputs are significance and security (love-unconditional and consistently

The Eye of the Believer

expressed; permanent acceptance" Crabb, L. (2014). This is what Pauls when explaining the grace and mercy of God toward all we who were undeserving.

"For scarcely for a righteous man will one die: yet peradventure for a good man some would even dare to die. But God commendeth his love toward us, in that, while we were yet sinners, Christ died for us."

Romans 5:7-8 KJV

If we will allow ourselves to see others in the light that God sees us, our attitude toward them would be much different.

Too often we view those who do not think like us as our enemies when that is not the case. Even if they differ completely from us in their thinking and belief system, that does not make them our enemies. Some have not come into the Light of the knowledge of God and we should make it our purpose to show them the love of God and pray for their understanding.

"That is why, ever since I heard of your strong faith in the Lord Jesus and of the love you have for Christians everywhere, I have never stopped thanking God for you. I pray for you constantly, asking God, the glorious Father of our Lord Jesus Christ, to give you the wisdom to see clearly and really understand who Christ is and all that he has done for you. I pray that your hearts will be flooded with light so that you can see something of the future he has called you to share. I want you to realize that God has been made rich because we who are Christ's have been given to him! I pray that you will begin to understand how incredibly great his power is to help those who believe him."

Ephesians 1:15-19 The Living Bible

The Eye of the Believer

When I first gave my life to christ I was full of so much church zeal that I went to church every night for about six months straight. I was a sophomore in college and was studying to become a psychiatrist. I often neglected my studies because I felt God knew my heart and would give me all the answers I needed. I did not know about the scripture " Faith without Works is dead" I simply lack the vision, foresight, and understanding to know that I had to set my priorities in order if I were to obtain my goal. I learned to be temperate and to properly balance all the things I had going on in my life.

As I grew in Christ, I gained a clearer understanding of the will and purpose of God in my life. I have learned how to better rightly divide God's word and become a more balanced Christian.

I was blessed and God was merciful toward me eventually allowing me to obtain several college degrees.

Another area that I lost sight of was personal relationships with family. I think this is an area where a lot of Christians get off track. They focus too much on the ritual of attending the church building, that they fail to understand the importance of building healthy relationships both at church, home, and in their communities.

I have known couples who attend church regularly but neglect their home life to the point the couple loses their connection with each other. As I

The Eye of the Believer

said earlier it is so important to maintain balance as a child of God.

When you and I will allow God to open our eyes to his great resources of blessing we then will walk in his fullness having access to an unlimited resource of his blessing.

"But be ye doers of the word, and not hearers only, deceiving your own selves. For if any be a hearer of the word and not a doer, he is like unto a man beholding his natural face in a glass: For he beholdeth himself, and goeth his way, and straightway forgetteth what manner of man he was."
James 1:22-24 KJV

While it is important to maintain proper church attendance it is equally as important to maintain a proper balance in the home.

To have a healthy home life families must take the time to invest in their relationships. Parents need to spend time together, with each other as well as with their children. If you are single get to know yourself, invest in yourself.

I can remember when I was young and single I would go visiting the sick in the hospital or nursing home every week. Find something constructive and productive to do with your time on a weekly basis.

As a Christian counselor, I often hear clients tell me when referring to their mate, children, family member, or even friend; "We do not talk like we use to . I then ask them, "what was it like when

The Eye of the Believer

you use to talk, what has changed?" The answer normally comes down to the individual does not see the person the way they use to.

A healthy relationship involves making adjustments in our life. Accepting people for who they are and allowing them to grow and change.

The biggest challenge in many relationships is the inability to handle conflict. You have one in the family that is ready to run to a fight while the other avoids conflict at all cost. Conflict is not always a bad thing in a relationship. Conflict can bring about healthy change if it is handled properly.

What's important is to handle conflict in good fighting. That means that you allow each other the right to disagree with the other and try to come to a mutual agreement that brings about a positive outcome for all parties involved.

Don't allow your vision of the relationship to become clouded by anger, bitterness, and resentment. Too often couples and family members allow things to cloud their view of the relationship such as anger, lack of finances, lust, greed, pride, as well as a host of other issues.

Real Christianity means you will come to see and understand that it is important to take care of the home. This includes loving their wife as Christ loved the church. Loving your wife includes providing for her and the children.

A word to the Minister. I have been told and I agree, your first ministry is at home. You can not get so involved in the ministry that you neglect your

The Eye of the Believer

home. I have talked with the children of Pastors, Evangelist, Preachers, and even Bishops who have told me their father or mother were so involved in helping other people that they neglected to minister to their own family. This has caused a lot of minister's kids to be turned off by the church. Lord help us to be able to see the full picture.

    The journey God has taken me on to correct my vision both spiritually and naturally has broadened my worldview and has caused me to have and show more compassion for others. My prayer is that the grace of God will lead you to a clearer view and understanding of the will of God for you, your family, your friends, and all loved ones in your life that you hold near and dear.

"For I know the thoughts that I think toward you, says the LORD, thoughts of peace and not of evil, to give you a future and a hope."
*   Jeremiah 21:11   NKJV*

The Eye of the Believer

References

Barclay, W. (1975). *The Gospel of John: Vol. 1. The Daily Study Bible Series* (Rev. ed.). Westminster Press.

Barker, K. L., & Kohlenberger, J. R. (1994). *Zondervan NIV Bible commentary: Expositor's Bible Commentary* (Abridged ed.). Zondervan Pub. House.

Carter, L. (1983). *The push-pull marriage: Learning and living the art of give-and-take.* Baker Book House.

Corey, G. (2013). *Theory and practice of counseling and psychotherapy* [SUPPRESSED] (9th ed.). Wadsworth/Cengage Learning.

Coxe, A. C., Clement, & Pseudo-Athanasius. (1981). *Fathers of the third and fourth centuries: The Twelve Patriarchs, excerpts and epistles, The Clementina, Apocrypha, Decretals, Memoirs of Edessa and Syriac Documents, Remains of the first ages* (American ed.). Wm. B. Eerdmans Pub.

Crabb, L. (2014). *Effective biblical counseling: A model for helping caring Christians become capable counselors.* Zondervan.

Foxe, J. (2001). *Foxe's Book of Martyrs: Updated and abridged.* Barbour.

Heitler, S., Ph.D. (2013, March 18). *Marriage Problems? Here's an 8-Step Rescue Plan.* Psychology Today. https://www.psychologytoday.com/us/blog/resolution-not-conflict/201303/marriage-problems-heres-8-step-rescue-plan

Jensen, I. L. (1981). *Jensen's Survey of the New Testament.* Moody.

Knowles, E. (1999). *The Oxford dictionary of quotations* (5th ed.). Oxford University Press.

Martin, G. (n.d.). *The Phrase Finder.* https://www.phrases.org.uk/meanings/beauty-is-in-the-eye-of-the-beholder.html#:~:text=Shakespeare's%20version%20of%20'Beauty%20is%20in%20the%20eye,Beauty%20is%20bought%20by%20judgement%20of%20the%20eye

TME., Knowles, E., & Partington, A. (1999). *The Oxford dictionary of quotations (Major new edition)* (5th ed.). Oxford University Press.

Walton, A., Ph.D. (2018). *The Window To Understanding And Building Healthy Relationships.* Walton Publishing.

Wise Sayings and Quotes. (2020). Wise Sayings. https://www.wisesayings.com/eyes-quotes/#ixzz6i3ZPwhgh

www.ingramcontent.com/pod-product-compliance
Lightning Source LLC
Chambersburg PA
CBHW052230230426
43666CB00034B/2579